THE SEARCH

ANNE FRANK HOUSE
in cooperation with the Jewish Historical Museum

THE SEARCH

Eric Heuvel | Ruud van der Rol | Lies Schippers

Esther's parents

Esther

Helena

Bob's parents

Bob

Esther and Daniel

Helena and Jeroen

Bob

7

Then you moved in next door to my grandmother?

Yes. Helena became my best friend.

Look Esther, my diary... go ahead, read it, really!

The Canter family lived a few doors down from us. They were also Jewish and had a son Bob.

Delicious... What is it?

A Dutch specialty. Want the recipe?

I had a crush on Bob.

Ooooh, he's coming this way...

No, he's going to train at the boxing school. Let's have a look?

There he is! Hey Bob!

Don't do...

BOKS GALA

Huuh?

POW!

Oops, sorry.

So much for that romance!

I quickly felt at home in the Netherlands.

Aren't you homesick?

At times. I mostly miss my grandparents.

SCHOOL

My father was given work in a hospital. We felt safe in the Netherlands. But Hitler was intent on war...

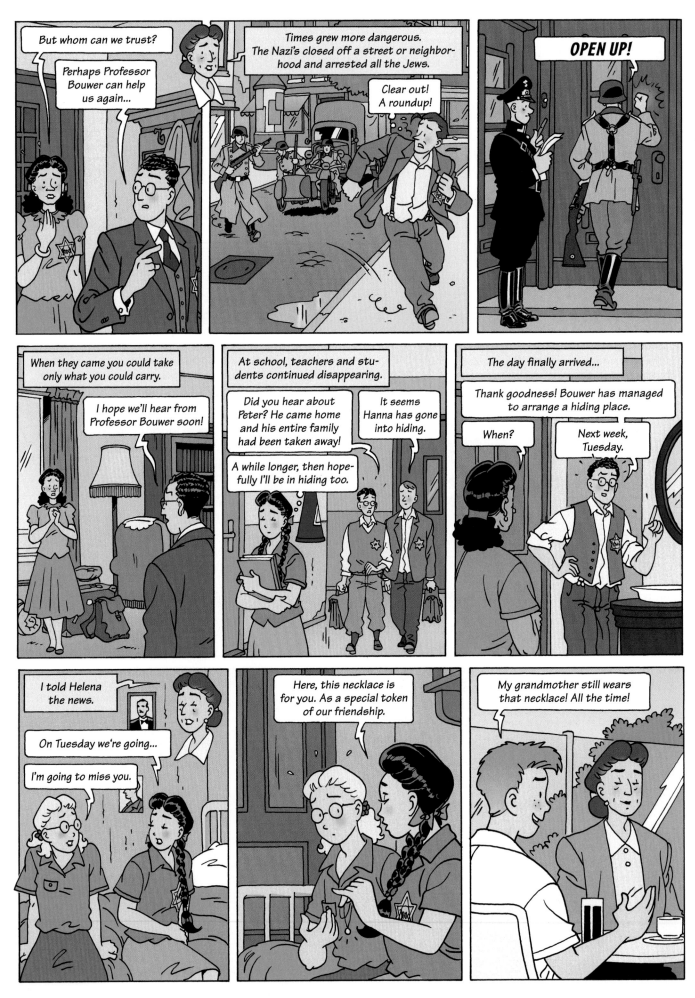

33

Farewell letters were thrown from the train. People who lived in the area often mailed them.

Dear Aunt and Uncle, We're in the train. We're very brave. So please don't worry. We have no idea where we're headed. Betty and Jacob.

How long is the trip?

I can't breathe!

No idea...

Don't push!

Careful! It's hard for her to stand.

Sit on these suitcases.

A day later...

The pail is full. The stench...

It can't be much longer.

After a while...

Empty the pails! Fetch water!

This isn't near over...

They were robbed on the way.

Your money and jewelry!

SCHNELL!

Three days later, everyone was totally exhausted.

So now, what's next?

They were on their way to Auschwitz, a death camp in occupied Poland.

The reality of what had gone on in Eastern Europe only became clear after the war.

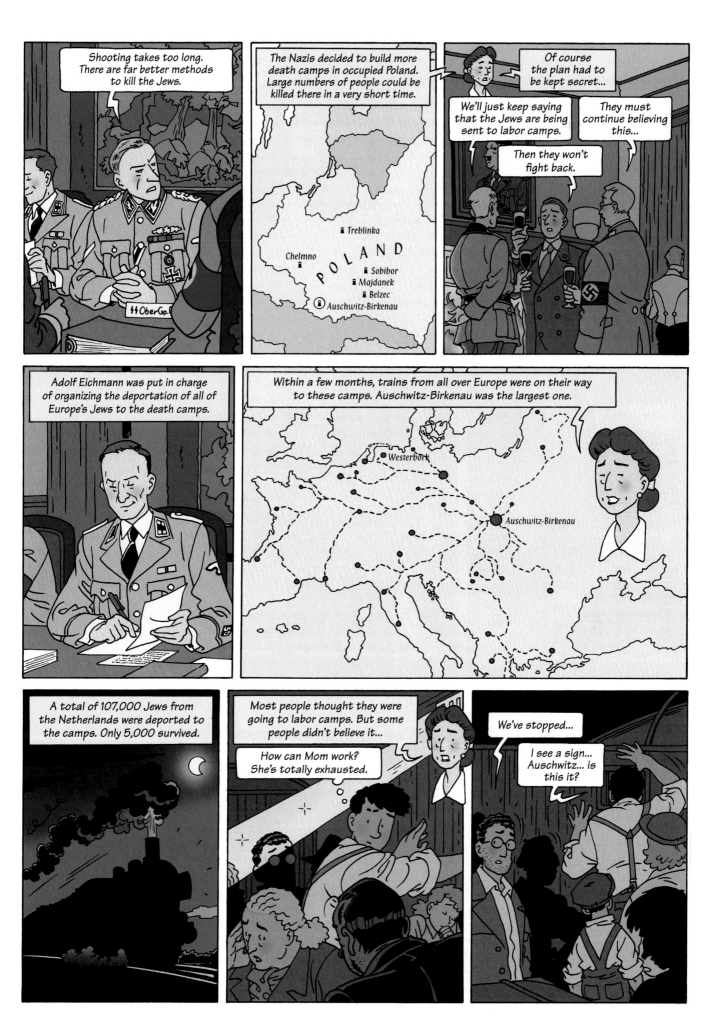

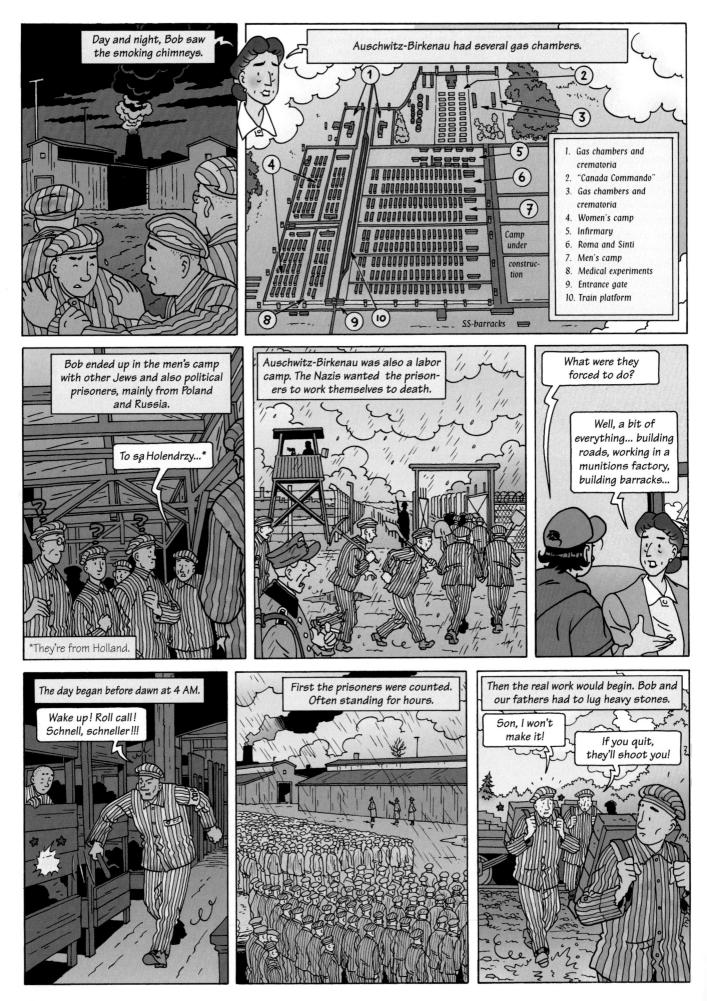

Day and night, Bob saw the smoking chimneys.

Auschwitz-Birkenau had several gas chambers.

1. Gas chambers and crematoria
2. "Canada Commando"
3. Gas chambers and crematoria
4. Women's camp
5. Infirmary
6. Roma and Sinti
7. Men's camp
8. Medical experiments
9. Entrance gate
10. Train platform

Camp under construction

SS-barracks

Bob ended up in the men's camp with other Jews and also political prisoners, mainly from Poland and Russia.

To są Holendrzy...*

*They're from Holland.

Auschwitz-Birkenau was also a labor camp. The Nazis wanted the prisoners to work themselves to death.

What were they forced to do?

Well, a bit of everything... building roads, working in a munitions factory, building barracks...

The day began before dawn at 4 AM.

Wake up! Roll call! Schnell, schneller!!!

First the prisoners were counted. Often standing for hours.

Then the real work would begin. Bob and our fathers had to lug heavy stones.

Son, I won't make it!

If you quit, they'll shoot you!

46

Scenario
Eric Heuvel
Ruud van der Rol
Lies Schippers
Drawings
Eric Heuvel / Redhill Illustrations
English Translation
Lorraine T. Miller / Epicycles
Coloring
J & M Colorstudio
Creative Support and Documentation
Jacqueline Koerts / Redhill Illustrations
Design
Karel Oosting
Production
Anne Frank House

A special thanks goes to Annemiek Gringold
(Hollandsche Schouwburg / Dutch Theatre Memorial Centre)
for contributing her expertise in the development
of the scenario.

The Search was originally published in Dutch as
De Zoektocht, thanks in part to funding provided by the
Ministry of Public Health, Welfare and Sport (VWS)
in the Netherlands.

Many others also offered their comments and advice
in the development of the scenario:

Content Experts (The Netherlands)
R.C. Musaph-Andriesse (Advisory Council, Anne Frank House);
Liesbeth van der Horst (Resistance Musem Amsterdam);
Dirk Mulder, Erik Guns (Memorial Center Camp Westerbork);
Nine Nooter (National Committee May 4th and 5th);
René Kok, Erik Somers (Netherlands Institute for War
Documentation / NIOD);
Jeroen van der Eijnde (National Monument Camp Vught);
Femke Akerboom (Markt 12 Museum, Aalten);
Ido Abram (Learning Foundation, Amsterdam);
Joost van Bodegom (Chairman Resistance Museum);
Joël Cahen, Petra Katzenstein, Léontine Meijer
(Jewish Historical Museum / Amsterdam);
Menno Metselaar, Marian Stegeman, Mieke Sobering
(Anne Frank House).

Content Experts (Abroad)
Paul Salmons (Imperial War Museum, Great Britain);
Wolf Kaiser (Wannsee Conference House Memorial, Germany);
Claude Singer and Philippe Boukara (Shoah Memorial, France);
Mirosław Obstarczyk (Auschwitz State Museum, Poland);
Piotr Trojanski (German-Polish Center, Poland);
Monica Kovács (Hannah Arendt Association, Hungary);
Werner Dreier (National Socialism and the Holocaust: Memory
and Present, Austria).

**Students and Teachers of Secondary School Programs
in the Netherlands**
C.S.G. Calvijn, Rotterdam; Christelijk Lyceum, Delft; Fioretti College,
Lisse; Gereformeerde SG Randstad, Rotterdam; Gomarus College,
Leeuwarden; Hartenlustschool, Bloemendaal; Havo Notre Dame
des Anges, Ubbergen; Kalsbeek College, Woerden; KSG De Breul,
Zeist; OSG De Meergronden, Almere; Pieter Nieuwland College
Amsterdam; Piter Jelles College, Leeuwarden; Prot. Chr. SG Groen
Van Prinsterer College, Barneveld; Schoter Scholengemeenschap,
Haarlem; Stebo, Den Haag; Strabrecht College, Geldrop;
Valuascollege, Venlo; Van der Capellen, S.G., Zwolle; Wellantcollege,
Alphen aan den Rijn; Wolvert Dalton, Rotterdam.